Old SMALL HEATH

by
John Bick

Small Heath station opened in 1863 and was originally called Small Heath & Sparkbrook. It was principally designed to serve the BSA works and was part of the Great Western Railway's Oxford line, opened in 1852. Services on this line now continue to London Marylebone. Trains on the North Warwickshire line (opened in 1907) bound for Stratford-upon-Avon also stop here. On the city side of the station marshalling yards with 27 lines were laid out.

© John Bick 2002
First published in the United Kingdom, 2002,
by Stenlake Publishing
Telephone / Fax: 01290 551122

ISBN 1 84033 232 8

The publishers regret that they cannot supply
copies of any pictures featured in this book.

The first record of 'Small Hethe' dates back to 1461 when it was part of the old parish of Aston. According to the caption this is a very early photograph of Green Lane, taken in 1890. By the early twentieth century both sides of the street had become completely built up.

The building in the centre between the shop awnings was originally called the Small Heath Tavern. It was renamed the Wrexham and latterly its name was changed to the Greenway, although most locals still called it the Wrexham. In the 1990s it was demolished to make way for a petrol station and supermarket.

3029. COVENTRY ROAD, SMALL HEATH.

Looking towards the city centre with Small Heath Park on the left. The shops on the right are still trading, but under different ownership. The gap between the buildings with a sign advertising Billingham's Whiskey [sic] once led to the steam tram depot but now provides access to a garage. Coventry Road used to be a turnpike road on which tolls were charged. A toll gate was erected near Green Lane corner in 1745 and the gate was removed when the road became free again in 1851.

The most striking thing about old postcards of Coventry Road – one of the main routes in and out of Birmingham – is the lack of traffic. As the main thoroughfare through Small Heath it commences at Bordesley, running eastwards through Hay Mills, South Yardley and Sheldon to the city boundary.

On 14 June 1931 a tornado struck Small Heath. After a very hot morning there was a torrential downpour of rain about 3.30 p.m., which was followed by the tornado. This picture of the corner of Coventry Road and Charles Road shows the damage that was caused to Boot's chemist's shop, which has got wooden slats nailed over its broken window.

This photograph was taken at the junction of Coventry Road and Wordsworth Road, opposite the spot where the picture on the facing page was taken. A hand-written message on the back says: 'Frazier's grocers near the park. Also the place where the motor car was blown through Boot's window.'

The off license at the corner of Green Lane and Victoria Street was seriously damaged by the tornado. Many houses and other buildings were wrecked too. In Small Heath park many trees and shrubs were uprooted, and greenhouses and plants destroyed.

This photograph was taken slightly further east along Green Lane. W. Osmond's butcher's shop on the corner of Palace Road (leading off to the right) is in the process of being repaired. One death resulted from the tornado when a lady was killed by falling masonry in Formans Road. The Lord Mayor of Birmingham set up a distress fund to raise money to help those whose property had been damaged.

Workmen breaking up the surface of Coventry Road in 1904 in preparation for the laying of new tram tracks. From 16 January 1886 double decker steam trams started running from the city centre to Small Heath park. Commencing on 29 March 1904, electric cars operated from the park across the city boundary to Church Road, Yardley. The gauge of the Birmingham trams was 3' 6" which was narrower than the standard gauge. This was stipulated by the Board of Trade which cited the narrowness of some of the streets the trams would have to pass down.

In this second view workmen are preparing the concrete foundation for the new tram tracks on Coventry Road. The Corporation relaid the track from Station Street to Church Road and the service on the new stretch commenced on 23 February 1905. Trams were numbered 15 and 16. The route was abandoned on Saturday 6 January 1934 and on the following morning trolleybuses Nos. 56 and 57 began running. The message on this postcard, franked 12 August 1904, reads: 'This is the state we are in all the way to town, but we are getting more tidy at Small Heath now'.

Coventry Road (alternatively known as Arthur Street) tram depot opened on 24 November 1905 and had room for 106 tramcars. It was on an awkward site, situated on a steep hill just below the point where the Stechford trams branched off up Cattell Road. The premises are now used by a lighting and sound design firm which hires out equipment for concert tours.

The Coventry Road tram depot cost more than £20,000 to build. In the early years of the twentieth century, until a new depot was built at Highgate Road, Stratford Road services such as this one originated from here. Birmingham had twenty tram depots, seven yards and 45 main routes totalling 80½ miles of track, making this the largest 3' 6" gauge system in the United Kingdom.

Looking down Coventry Road towards town with the tram depot on the left. This hill is known locally as Kingston hill; the Kingston cinema (now used as a community centre for the local Pentecostal church) was built in 1935 where the trees stand on the right. Up until the First World War Birmingham trams had letters with different coloured backgrounds to denote their destinations. Route numbers were introduced on 25 January 1915 in response to reduced levels of street lighting during wartime. The shops on the right of this picture have been demolished and a car park fronting Birmingham City's ground now occupies the site. Small Heath artist Thomas Wood Downing (1849–1931) lived in a Georgian house on Kingston hill which stood on the site later occupied by the cinema. Downing was known for his etchings of Birmingham street scenes and paintings of local farms. When he got married in 1881 he moved to 42 Golden Hillock Road.

At one time Small Heath had more cinemas than any other Birmingham district. This is the Grange on the corner of Coventry Road and Grange Road. It originally opened in 1915, but was rebuilt and reopened in May 1922 shortly before the Coronet opened just down the road from it. Known in full as the Grange Super Cinema, it had a seating capacity of 1,310 and the proprietors were Coronet Cinema. It closed on 31 October 1959, with *April Love* starring Pat Boone and Shirley Jones the last film to be shown.

A second view of the same stretch of Coventry Road, again showing the Grange cinema. The enormous Birmingham Industrial Co-operative Society premises in the foreground incorporated ten shops at this branch, No. 2. Tram No. 113, built by United Electric in 1907 and operating service 16 to Yardley, is travelling towards the camera.

The shop in the middle distance on the corner of Regent Park Road is that of H. G. Turner Ltd., corn merchant. The business was established in 1884 and still trades in Coventry Road. A stone plaque above the shops on the right reads 'Arthur Place, 1867'.

Coventry Road at the junction with Whitmore Road (left) and Grange Road (right). The ornate tower beyond the Grange Road junction belonged to the Wesleyan Methodist Church, which was demolished in the 1960s.

Looking in the opposite direction to the previous picture, this view also shows the Wesleyan Methodist Church (built in 1876). An Aldi supermarket now occupies its site. Jenkins Street is on the right.

Cyril Road runs from Coventry Road to Henshaw Road. The latter was named after Frederick Henry Henshaw (1807–1891), an artist who lived in the cottage adjacent to Green Lane Farm. He became a member of the Royal Society of Artists in 1840 and an exhibition of his work was held in the city art gallery in 1888.

Langley Road at the Glover's Road end looking towards Coventry Road.

This postcard was sent in 1940 during the dark days of World War II. Charles Road is on the right, with the branch of Boot's that got damaged in the tornado on the corner. Nearer the camera on the right with its sun blinds open is Foster Bros.' clothiers.

Looking away from the city along Coventry Road with Charles Road on the left and Wordsworth Road to the right. Note the delivery man struggling to lift goods from his van to a sack truck.

St Oswalds Road is on the left of this picture of Coventry Road, with the park on the right. All the houses illustrated here have been turned into shops. A plaque high up on the wall at the centre of the terrace reveals they were built in 1886.

In 1876 Miss Louisa Ryland presented 41 acres of her Small Heath estate on Coventry Road to the city for use as a park. Work on laying it out began the same year and the park was officially opened by the Mayor of Birmingham on 5 April 1879. This picture shows the refreshment rooms, one of many amenities in the park when the postcard was sent in 1908. These also included tennis courts, a bowling green and a pond.

The park keeper's lodge is still standing but has been boarded up for several years. On 23 March 1887, during her golden jubilee year, Queen Victoria came to Birmingham to open the law courts in Corporation Street and en route visited Small Heath park. A local holiday was proclaimed to celebrate the occasion and no public transport ran between 10 a.m. and 3 p.m. The Queen arrived by royal train at Small Heath station and entered the park by carriage through the Wordsworth Road gate. Schoolchildren from the city and further afield had gathered to witness the visit, and lined the route from Wordsworth Road gate to Coventry Road gate to cheer the Queen.

Following Queen Victoria's visit, the council asked for permission to change the park's name to Victoria Park, which explains the caption on this postcard. The request was granted, although I have never heard it called Victoria Park.

St Oswald's Road, with St Oswald's church on the right. This brick and stone building was erected and consecrated in 1893, but St Oswald's originated in 1882 as a mission church attached to St Andrew's, Bordesley, when it was housed in an iron building. It got parish church status in 1899. The former church is now used as a Muslim preparatory school for boys and girls aged four to eleven.

The houses in Dora Road have changed little since this postcard was sent in 1909. Some have had porches added, or their front gardens paved for parking, and the lean-to structure in the foreground of this picture has been demolished.

Mansell Road, like several others in the area, is named after a member of the Digby family, who at one time were the principal landowners in the district.

26

Heather Road is another road named after a member of the Digby family, landowners who sold their estate in Small Heath for development.

These houses in Oldknow Road were bomb-damaged in March 1940. Like other parts of the city Small Heath experienced its fair share of damage. Over 2,500 people were killed in air-raids on Birmingham during the Second World War and many more were injured. A severe raid caused great loss of life at the nearby BSA factory during this period.

There are plenty of horse droppings in this photograph of Oldknow Road. I used to collect horse manure from the streets with a bucket and spade and sell it to gardeners – allotment owners in particular were very keen to buy it and paid 2*d*. per bucket.

Armoury Road is on the boundary of Small Heath. The factory on the right was part of the famous Birmingham Small Arms (BSA) Co. This was formed in 1861 when a 25 acre site was bought at Small Heath. The first factory had been built by 1868 and at the time was the largest private arms factory in Europe. In 1879, because of falling demand for arms, the company diversified into cycle manufacture and by 1913 had become the largest bicycle and motorbike manufacturer in the country. During the First World War output was converted entirely to arms production, and every Lewis gun used by British troops was made by BSA. Between the wars BSA expanded, acquiring several other companies. The range of products manufactured included machine tools, cars and light engineering products. During the Second World War BSA reverted to making armaments and after the war further expansion took place. However, decline followed and the company had gone out of business by 1973. By the 1980s the Armoury Road works had been demolished and the BSA industrial park now occupies its site.

Malmesbury Road runs from Coventry Road to Waverley Road. The chimney belongs to the BSA.

Well-to-do middle class housing on Tennyson Road. The houses in Tennyson Road are very fine and were built for the professional classes. I lived in one for a short time during the 1950s. Because of their size most have now been turned into flats. Small Heath Park is on the right.

This tram, travelling down Byron Road, is on the No. 22 Bolton Road service which terminated at Waverley Road near the BSA factory. Being only about 1½ miles long the route was never financially viable, and was abandoned on 5 February 1930. It had opened on 1 January 1907 and this postcard was sent in September of that year.

Another view of Byron Road, showing the overhead cables for the No. 22 service. The building on the left, with the horse and cart outside, is the old Waverley School, built in 1892. This became a secondary school in 1933 and a grammar school in 1945. In 1965 the school moved to new premises in Hobmoor Road and the building is currently used as a sixth form centre.

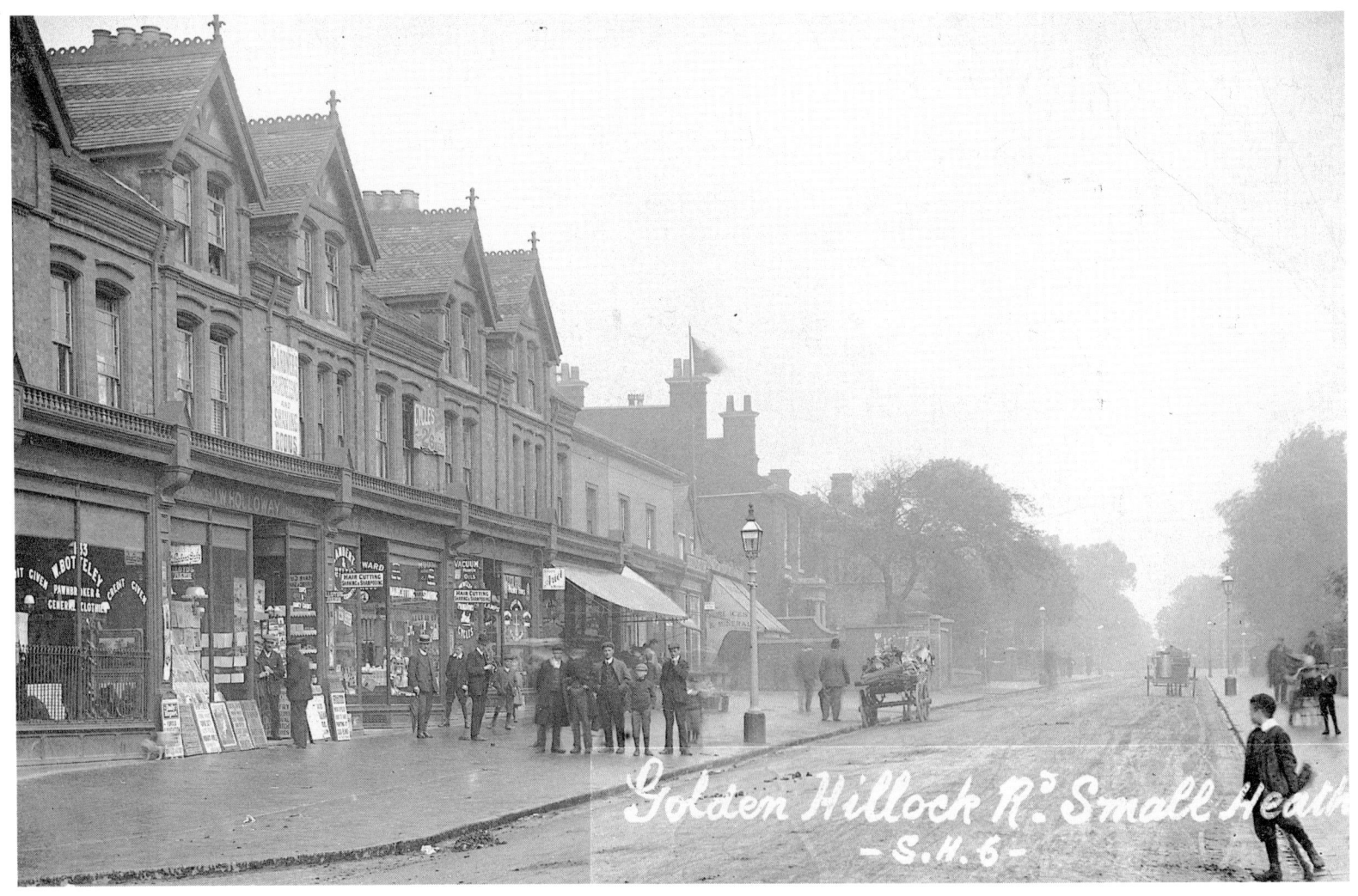

Golden Hillock Road looking towards Coventry Road, with the shop at No. 133, home to a pawnbrokers, in the left foreground. Beyond the pawnshop is a newsagents, followed by a hairdressers and what appears to be a cycle shop. These shops lay just beyond the junction of Bolton Road and have all now been demolished.

A second view of Golden Hillock Road, looking in the same direction but showing the stretch of road opposite the shops seen in the previous picture. All the buildings shown have been demolished to make way for the bypass road and mosque which now occupy this vicinity.

Golden Hillock Road with a horse-drawn railway van travelling towards Coventry Road. The shop with the blind down is J. Hedges' bakers and confectioners which later became part of the Birmingham Co-op. On the left is the junction of Glover's Road and Cooksey Road. Although the houses are still standing the trees have gone, as have all the railings, along with some of the walls they are standing on.

Green Lane stretches for about a mile, and this picture was taken about halfway along its length looking east towards Blake Lane. The shop in the left foreground at No. 314, just beyond the junction with Palace Road, was occupied by Joseph Mottram, butcher. Frederick Henshaw, an artist, owned land in the vicinity of Green Lane and would not allow any houses to be built on his estate. He died in 1891 and the land was divided up and developed for building from about 1898.

Green Lane looking west, with Mansel Road on the left – I used to play football in the roads around here. As a schoolboy I was a paper boy for Wright's newsagents in Green Lane and delivered papers to houses in Yardley Green Road and the top end of Belcher's Lane. Years later as a postman I delivered mail to the same addresses.

Green Lane, Small Heath.

Looking west along Green Lane, with Hobmoor Road on the left and Blake Lane to the right. When I went shopping with my mother during the 1930s and 40s, the Co-op occupied both of the corner sites shown here. The greengrocers was on the corner of Blake Lane, with the general grocers opposite on the corner of Hobmoor Road, adjoined by the butchers and bakery. This crossroads is the highest point in Small Heath, being 435 feet above sea level.

Charles Road runs from Coventry Road across Green Lane before reaching the main thoroughfare of Bordesley Green. Although the houses shown here are still standing, their railings have been removed, probably in the drive for scrap metal during the Second World War. The shop on the corner has adverts for Cadbury's chocolate and Rountree's cocoa on its walls.

Somerville Road runs from Muntz Street to Haybarnes Road. The Haybarnes Road end was not built up until the 1920s.

Floyer Road. The Digby estate was developed from the 1880s onwards, and Floyer, Charles, Bankes, Dora, Hugh, Kenelm, Mansel, Somerville and Venetia Roads are among those street names with connections to the Digby family.

Aubrey Road was named after another member of the Digby family. Digby Park is visible at the end of the street.

The fence on the right surrounds St Benedict's Church, while the junction beyond is that of Bankes Road. The picture was taken looking downhill towards Coventry Road.

Hobmoor Road runs from the east end of Green Lane to Yew Tree Lane, Yardley. This picture was taken at the Green Lane end looking towards the River Cole. Hobmoor Road is named after the farm of the same name. During the 1920s many farms in the area were purchased by the city council for the building of municipal housing estates.

In the early years of the twentieth century the Amateur Gardeners' Club was situated at 2–4 Blake Lane. However, in 1923 it moved to these premises in Hobmoor Road which it still occupies today. This once very popular club formerly had a waiting list of several years for membership.

Hob-Moor Road, Small Heath.

The building behind the trees on the left of this picture of Hobmoor Road is St Benedict's Church, consecrated in 1910. It is now a grade 2 listed building.

HOB MOOR LANE YARDLEY

This ford over the River Cole marks the border between Small Heath and Yardley; until November 1911 the river also formed the county boundary between Warwickshire and Worcestershire. The housing estates now covering this area were built in the 1920s. The name Hobmoor dates from the sixteenth century and Hobmoor Lane once led to several farms; the ford across the River Cole lay beyond the farms. At this point there was a dog-leg in the lane and anyone crossing the ford with a wagon and horses had to travel along the riverbed for about 100 yards before turning into the lane again. Hobmore Lane (now Hobmoor Road) was realigned and a bridge built *c.*1926.